# SKIN & LIARS

## DENNIS FOON

**Playwrights Canada**
**Toronto**

**Playwrights Canada Press** is the publishing imprint of
the Playwrights Union of Canada (PUC): 54 Wolseley St., 2nd fl.
Toronto, Ontario CANADA M5T 1A5
Tel: (416) 703-0201 Fax: (416) 703-0059



**Playwrights Canada Press** operates with the generous assistance of The Canada Council - Writing and Publishing Section, and Theatre Section, the Ontario Arts Council, and the Ontario Publishing Centre.

*Cover photo by David Cooper.*

**Canadian Cataloguing in Publication Data**
Foon, Dennis 1951 —
Skin & liars
Two plays
ISBN 0-88754-468-1
I. Title.II Title:Liars
PS8561.065S55 1988 jC812'.54 C88-094946-5
PR9199.3.F66S55 1988

First edition: September 1988
Second printing: September 1993
Third printing: August 1995
Printed and bound in Winnipeg, Manitoba, Canada.

# CONTENTS

## FOREWORD

Canada is my adopted home and Vancouver my adopted city. I am often asked why I came here. The answer to that question also explains why the plays in this volume were written.

When I was growing up in Detroit I used to spend my summers in Algonquin Park, Ontario. The tranquility of those lakes and forests always served as an antidote to the tumult in my home town. One summer, when I came back from canoeing, I found out that Detroit was burning. Our house was only a few miles from Twelfth Street—I had no idea whether the rioting had reached my neighborhood or not.

It hadn't—but the repercussions had. When I returned to high school that fall, the tension was unbearable. Coley High was half white, half black—and ready to blow up. It did. One day, sitting in english class, we heard a sound like thunder coming from the hallway. The teacher looked out the window and said, "Class dismissed." The thunder was the sound of people running. And the sound of people being beaten. Groups of blacks on whites, groups of whites on blacks. When I got outside all over the schoolgrounds were little hills of people, pummeling each other. All I remember is running and running, trying to escape from the insanity.

Some years later, when I was invited to pursue my MFA at the University of British Columbia, I jumped at the chance. I hated Detroit, hated the fact that things had become so polarized, so far gone that I couldn't see an end to the social problems. And of course, Canada had always represented a kind of Mecca to me. I had always sworn I'd get here somehow.

When I finished my degree and we started Green Thumb Theatre, I had little idea in the beginning what theatre for young people could be. But very soon it became clear to me that theatre could be a way to communicate ideas, a way to work toward change.

By comparision with the violence and chaos in Detroit, Vancouver was a very calm and sensible place. But it was clear that the seeds of many of the same problems that I experienced in Detroit were pervasive in Canada. To me they are like St. Exupery's Baobab seeds: if we ignore them, they will destroy us.

The characters in these plays are fictional but their experiences are not invented. Their stories were told to me again and again by youth living in Vancouver and Toronto.

Canada is a progressive country and its record with race relations, for example, is not all that bad when compared to other countries. But clearly there is much work to be done: problems need to be addressed, not denied.

I believe in the possibility for change and I believe that it is up to each of us to make it happen, both inside and outside. These plays are a vote for the future.

Dennis Foon
*August, 1988*

# SKIN

The script of *Skin* published here is the "Toronto" version, which was first produced in that city by Young People's Theatre in April, 1986, with the following cast:

| | |
|---|---|
| JENNIFER; BLONDE; SPONSOR; MRS. PAUL | *Janet Bailey* |
| TODD; LO; MR. LIZARD; HUNK; COP | *Henry Czerny* |
| TUAN; SHOPKEEPER | *Robert Lee* |
| PHIROZA; DELACY; WHITE GIRL | *Debbie Sall* |

*Directed by Dennis Foon.*
*Designed by Marti Wright.*
*Masks by Katherine Hahn.*
*Stage Managed by Kate Greenway.*

The "Vancouver" version of *Skin* was first produced by Green Thumb Theatre in March, 1986, with the following cast:

| | |
|---|---|
| KAREN; BLONDE; SPONSOR; MRS. PAUL | *Lori Lewis* |
| TODD; LO; MR. LIZARD; HUNK; COP | *Thomas Hunt* |
| TUAN; SHOPKEEPER | *Keeman Wong* |
| PHIROZA; SABRINA; WHITE GIRL | *Zena Daruwalla* |

*Directed by Dennis Foon.*
*Designed by Marti Wright.*
*Masks by Katherine Hahn.*
*Stage Managed by Erin Hubert.*

The "Vancouver" version of *Skin* is available from the agent, Green Thumb Theatre. In it, the character JENNIFER Malcolm is replaced by KAREN Williams, of the Leelwat People.

The Characters

PHIROZA Mehta
JENNIFER Malcolm
TUAN Hung Wong
DELACY
MR. LIZARD
LO
TODD
*Tuan's* SPONSOR
MRS. PAUL, *Tuan's Supervisor*
SHOPKEEPER
COP
WHITE GIRL
*Various* "Mask" *Figures*

Staging Notes

*Skin may be performed by as few as four actors — the three principal characters and one male actor.*

*The set in the original production was made up of a series of platforms with several cut-out silhouettes of human figures. On the left side of the stage stood a set of lockers which were used by* PHIROZA, MRS. PAUL *and* MR. LIZARD, *who would pop up behind them and use them as his podium and playing area.*

## PLAYWRIGHT'S NOTE

*The development of this script was made possible by Project One (Judith Mastai, Project Director) and Young People's Theatre (Peter Moss, Artistic Director). Project One was co-sponsored by International Briefing Associates Inc. and the Vancouver East Cultural Centre.*

*The assistance of Multiculturalism Canada, Canadian Employment and Immigration, the Alma Van Dusen Fund—BC Conference, United Church of Canada, the City of Vancouver and the Ontario Arts Council is gratefully acknowledged.*

*I owe particular thanks to the participants of the two Project One workshops: Judith Mastai, Jane Heyman, Etsuko Yamanouchi, Edward Hong-Louie, Ruby Truly, Steven So, David Marr and a giant thank you to Zena Daruwalla for allowing me to fictionalize some of her life experiences in order to create the character* PHIROZA.

*In creating Skin, my hope was to tell three specific stories that would break stereotypes and shed light on the range of ways racism affects kids' lives. During my research I found that one of the most prevalent forms of institutionalized discrimination takes place in the education system, simply through the underestimation of a young person's potential. This undervaluing can become a self-fulfilling prophecy, and has had a devastating impact on countless visible minorities.*

*After months of research and hundreds of interviews, I have come to the conclusion that while the specifics of each person's experience is unique, the formula by which institutionalized racism touches people is not unique at all.* MR. LIZARD *is alive and well and living throughout Canada.*

*This play is dedicated to all those people working to make Canada a truly free and equal society.*

## Scene One

| | |
|---|---|
| ACTOR 1 | I am five foot six inches tall. |
| ACTOR 2 | I weigh 150 pounds. |
| ACTOR 3 | I have two arms |
| ACTOR 4 | Two legs |
| ACTOR 1 | Two feet |
| ACTOR 2 | Two ears |
| ACTOR 3 | Two eyes |
| ACTOR 4 | One nose |
| ACTOR 1 | One mouth |
| ACTOR 2 | Ten fingers |
| ACTOR 3 | Ten toes. |
| ACTOR 4 | I can taste |
| ACTOR 1 | I can smell |
| ACTOR 2 | I can see |
| ACTOR 3 | I can hear |

| | |
|---|---|
| ACTOR 4 | I can touch |
| ACTOR 1 | My blood is red |
| ACTOR 2 | My blood is red |
| ACTOR 3 | My blood is red |
| ACTOR 4 | My blood is red. |
| ACTOR 1 | I breathe. |
| ACTOR 2 | I think. |
| ACTOR 3 | I feel. |
| ACTOR 4 | I feel. |
| ACTOR 1 | I feel. |
| ACTOR 2 | I feel. |

## Scene Two

PHIROZA My name is Phiroza Mehta. In persian, Phiroza means Victorious. In gudjerati, Mehta means Teacher. I was born in Bombay. It's on the west coast of India. My dad worked for Air India and traveled all over the world. So when I was four years old, he and my mom decided to take the family and move. So we sat down in that fat jumbo jet and 19 hours later landed in Toronto. It was so cold I thought my ears would fall off.

JENNIFER My name is Jennifer Malcolm. The name Jennifer comes from Gwenevere, the wife of King Arthur. In Celtic, it means The White One. The name Malcolm comes from latin—it means White Dove. So on paper, anyway, I'm very white. My dad's an engineer and comes from Jamaica. My mom's from Trinidad—she works in a bookstore. I was born in Toronto, Ontario.
I love rock music.
Loud.

TUAN My name is Wong Tuan Hung (pronounced: Wun Hungh Dwon). In chinese, my name means many things. I was born in Hanoi, North Vietnam. My father is Chinese, my mother Vietnamese. When the conflict started between China and Vietnam, it was very hard for us to live. My parents thought it would be safer if we left the country for a while but they only had enough money to send my older brother, my younger sister and me. My parents stayed behind.

When we left Vietnam there were 300 of us in a 30 metre boat. It was pretty crowded. When half of us slept, the other half stood to make room. We floated for over half a month. We kept asking ships from different countries to tow us to the mainland but they wouldn't get involved. Besides, they said, we weren't in any danger—the boat was still floating. But then it sank, so we were given help. About 60 people drowned, though. Including my older brother.

## Scene Three

PHIROZA When I was growing up we lived outside Toronto and I was friendly with everybody. At the elementary school I went to everybody played together. Most of the kids were born here but their grandparents came from other countries. But then we moved and I started going to a different school.

*One of the actors explodes a paper lunch bag.*

What did you call me?

*Another explosion.*

I'm from India.

*Another.*

Listen, Pakistan and India are two different countries.

*Another.*

I'm a Parsi, Parsis are Zoroastrians, one of the world's oldest religions...we even had an influence on the bible because—

*Another.*

Look, I'm from Bombay, in the state of Maharashtra.

*Another.*

Listen, there are a lot of states in India.

*Another.*

They didn't care who I really was or where I really came from. Because as far as they were concerned, there was no such thing as *me* anymore.

## Scene Four

JENNIFER — You know, for a long time I was really happy. I loved the school I went to, I found it really easy. That was good, cause I loved to party. Friday, concerts, Saturdays, parties. The school was great, everybody hung out together, it didn't matter what colour you were—white, black, purple—I never had any problems cause I was black. I didn't think anybody really did—except for my cousin Delacy.

DELACY *is chuckling.*

DELACY — The strangest thing happened this morning.

JENNIFER — What, Delacy?

DELACY — I got on the bus this morning, sat next to this white lady. She jumps up and starts walking away.

JENNIFER — Maybe it was her stop.

DELACY — Yeah, I wondered about that—so I followed her.

JENNIFER You did?

DELACY Uh huh. And you know what? She sat down someplace else.

JENNIFER So what did you do?

DELACY Sat down next to her again. And you know what?

JENNIFER What?

DELACY Her face completely changed: her nose turned bright red and then the colour spread to her cheeks and then her ears lit up.

JENNIFER Maybe she thought you had rabies.

DELACY Maybe she thought my colour would rub off on her.

JENNIFER Maybe it had nothing to do with you at all.

DELACY Right, Jennifer.

JENNIFER There could be a million reasons other than that you're black.

DELACY You really think so, Jennifer?

JENNIFER Yes, Delacy. Yes...

## Scene Five

PHIROZA — Sometimes I'm not sure which is worse—getting called names and pushed around—or just being invisible. It's amazing how people can make you feel like you're not really there.

*Mask mime.*

*Music, upbeat. For example, The Pointer Sisters' "Jump."*

PHIROZA *sits centre, perhaps with magazine, as if she is in some kind of waiting room.*

*Female mask figure (*BLONDE*) enters, dancing. Her mask is simply a beautiful smiling teen model's face (bigger than lifesize) cut out of a magazine.*

*The* BLONDE *sits.* PHIROZA *smiles at her. The* BLONDE *looks at* PHIROZA *with her frozen grin, then looks forward, tapping to the music.*

PHIROZA *looks at her, trying to initiate a conversation but the* BLONDE *keeps looking forward, so* PHIROZA *goes back to her magazine in frustration.*

*Pause.*

*Another mask figure enters, dancing. A male.*

*His mask is also a full size magazine cutout. A current teenage heartthrob, grinning. We'll call him* HUNK.

*He sees the* BLONDE, *does a few moves and sits next to* PHIROZA.

PHIROZA *smiles and nods at him. He glances at her, nods with his frozen smile.*

PHIROZA *smiles. They both look forward.*

HUNK *turns away.* PHIROZA *looks at him, smiling.*

*The* BLONDE *looks at* HUNK.

PHIROZA, *still smiling, turns and realizes that* HUNK *isn't looking at her, but at* BLONDE.

PHIROZA *sits uncomfortably.*

*Pause.*

HUNK *looks at* BLONDE.

BLONDE *looks at* HUNK.

*They stare at each other.*

*Pause.* PHIROZA *withers.*

*He nods.*

*She nods.*

*He shrugs.*

*She shrugs.*

*They both stand up.*

*She takes his arm and they exit, dancing.*

Believe me, you don't need science fiction to become the Invisible Man.

## Scene Six

---

TUAN

My sister was 12, I was 16. We were taken to Hong Kong where we stayed in a camp with other refugees. It was hard in the camp. Many people were cruel to use because they thought we were Vietnamese. But we left Vietnam because they were hard on us for being Chinese. Sometimes it is very difficult to understand the way people behave... But then a church in Canada sponsored us and we came here. When we first came off the plane, our sponsors were there to meet us. But no one spoke chinese or vietnamese so it was very confusing.

*The* SPONSOR *enters. She is holding a snapshot, looking for someone. She sees* TUAN. *She carefully walks over to* TUAN, *trying to see if the photo and face match. As she cranes to look,* TUAN *turns. She quickly looks away.*

*Slight pause.*

*The* SPONSOR *tries to sneak another look at* TUAN, *but he looks at her so she turns away.*

*The* SPONSOR *tries to sneak another look but this time* TUAN *catches her. She smiles.*

SPONSOR Are you Tuan?

TUAN, *not understanding, just looks at her.*

Tuan?

TUAN, *hearing this appalling pronounciation of his name, tentatively points to himself.*

TUAN Tuan?

SPONSOR, *thinking it might be him, points to the snapshot.*

SPONSOR Tuan?

TUAN (*happily*) Tuan!

SPONSOR (*relieved*) Tuan! Hello, I am your sponsor.

TUAN, *of course, does not understand and just looks at her.*

*Pause.*

(*loudly*) Hello! *I am your sponsor!*

TUAN (*smiles and nods; then, to audience*) Why do people think you'll understand if they say it louder?

SPONSOR (*very loud*) Me Sponsor. You Tuan!

TUAN But our sponsors were very nice. They really wanted to help. But we were quite confused. Their house was different from any we had ever seen. And the food was strange. Our first day of school we were given lunchboxes. (*holds up a ridiculous lunchbox*) It seemed like an odd way to carry food. English classes take place in an annex outside the school. To get to the main office, I had to go through the front hallway. It was full of kids.

*The other actors put on neutral masks. They sit upstage of* TUAN. *He enters their area. They look up. He stops. Speaks in halting english.*

Excuse me... Office? ...office?

*Pause.*

Office.

TUAN *starts to cross.*

*The first figure quickly stands, blocking* TUAN*'s path.*

TUAN *hesitates. The figure moves toward him.* TUAN *backs away.*

*The figure and* TUAN *stand face to face. Suddenly, the figure raises his arm and smashes* TUAN*'s book out of his hands.*

TUAN *moves slowly away from the figure and picks up his book.*

*The figures stand watching him.*

That was my first and last visit to the front hallway.

*The figures exit.* TUAN *starts to sit with his book.* LO *enters.*

[*Playwright's note: most of the* TUAN/LO *scenes begin and end with them speaking in cantonese together. The speeches are written in rough phonetics with an english translation in brackets.*]

LO — Nay mo see ah mah? [Are you okay?]

TUAN — Mo see. [No problem.]

LO — Are you all right?

TUAN — (*to audience*) This was Lo. Lo became my first friend in Canada. He was Chinese and from Vietnam, just like me. And he was someone I could really talk to—in my own language.

She na gnah mm shi da gow. [They were just giving me a hard time.]

LO — Why didn't you fight?

TUAN — I've seen enough blood. I've seen enough death. We've both seen war.

LO — It's a war here too.

TUAN — Oh, yeah? Where are the bombs? The bodies on the ground? You call this war?

LO In a way. You think they like you?

TUAN Those guys don't. But it's not the same for all of them.

LO Yes it is. Half of them give us a hard time and the other half let them do it. Not one new student can walk through that hallway. They all walk around the block so they can sneak in the back door. And the teachers don't see a thing.

TUAN Get off it.

LO It's true.

TUAN We've been through this before, Lo. There are a lot of people here on our side.

LO And a lot who aren't.

TUAN So?

LO You've got to stick up for yourself...I push you, you push me back. (*pushes* TUAN)

TUAN Lo, quit playing games.

LO (*pushing* TUAN *again*) Those guys are gonna waste you.

TUAN No chance.

LO I'll teach you.

LO *goes to push* TUAN *again, but this time* TUAN *suddenly attacks him, locks* LO*'s arm in a hold, with his hand at* LO*'s throat.*

TUAN — I know how to fight. You know I know how to fight.

LO *breaks the hold; they both leap into fighting stances.*

LO — Then come on!

TUAN — (*breaking from his fighting stance*) ...no.

LO — What's stopping you?

TUAN — After all I've been through to get here, I can't afford to get into trouble now—I have to work. I have to get my parents out of Vietnam.

LO — Then you have to fight. My whole family is depending on me to save them too—and I will. What about you?

TUAN — I'll help them. I have to. But I don't have to fight. Ngoh mh sai tong koyee day dah gow. [I don't have to fight.]

LO — Ho-ah! [Okay!] Joy geen. [See you around.]

## Scene Seven

PHIROZA — I guess it was last June, all of a sudden it was summer. It was just the crummiest weather and out of nowhere: Sun. I put on my shorts and shades, got on my old bike and headed for the beach...so I'm on this quiet street when I pass these guys and the biggest one of them, who looks like the Terminator, yells at me: "Hey you—Blah, Blah!" I was paralyzed for a second, scared. I was minding my own business, what did I do? Then something snapped. What right did he have to ruin my day? So then I looked him right in the eye, and as loud as I could yelled: BLAH BLAH YOURSELF! They just froze. Six evil looking guys with their mouths dropped open and eyes bugged out, like this: (*demonstrates*) I guess they were a little surprised.

## Scene Eight

JENNIFER Like I said, school was really a cinch. All my teachers were really nice too. Except for one—Mr. Lizard.

MR. LIZARD *slowly enters, his green clawed hands emerging first. He wears a sports jacket and tie and has a very green lizard mask. He sees a fly. Swats it out of the air and eats it with gusto.*

MR. LIZARD Passing notes again, Miss Malcolm?

JENNIFER No, Mr. Lizard.

MR. LIZARD I saw you passing notes, Miss Malcolm.

JENNIFER But sir—

MR. LIZARD No buts. Out. You. Go.

JENNIFER Or he'd—

MR. LIZARD What was so funny about that, Miss Malcolm?

JENNIFER Nothing, Mr. Lizard.

MR. LIZARD Then why were you laughing?

JENNIFER I wasn't laughing, sir.

MR. LIZARD Then what did I hear?

JENNIFER I don't know, sir.

MR. LIZARD Out. You. Go.

JENNIFER Mr. Lizard always singled me out, I didn't know why. He considered me a loser.

MR. LIZARD You, Miss Malcolm, have an atrocious attitude toward the learning process.

JENNIFER I do?

MR. LIZARD You are lazy. You don't have what it takes.

JENNIFER That's not fair.

MR. LIZARD It's an objective assessment.

JENNIFER No it's not.

MR. LIZARD Are you being smart with me, young lady?

JENNIFER Yes, that's exactly what I am, smart. I'm a lot smarter than you think.

MR. LIZARD Out. You. Go.

MR. LIZARD *exits.*

DELACY — You know, he did the same thing to me when I was in his class.

JENNIFER — Really, Delacy?

DELACY — The old Lizard of Oz used to pick on me all the time too.

JENNIFER — He did?

DELACY — All he figured I was good for was athletics. Come to think of it, a lot of my teachers thought I was definite sports material.

JENNIFER — You? Why?

DELACY — Beats me. Funny, though, nobody ever encouraged me to be a scientist. Anybody ever encourage you?

JENNIFER — No.

DELACY — Come to think of it—why are you in vocational school?

JENNIFER — Because my counselor thought it was a good idea.

DELACY — If your counselor thought it was a good idea, would you jump in a lake?

JENNIFER — Not if it was Lake Erie.

DELACY — You're smart—smart enough to go to university. Why aren't you in a collegiate?

JENNIFER — Cause I'm lazy.

DELACY That's what Mr. Lizard says. But I've seen how hard you can work when you're interested in something. You're not lazy.

JENNIFER I am at school.

DELACY Maybe they're boring you. If you tried, you could go to university. You should.

JENNIFER No way. (*to audience*) But I wondered about that. Why was I doing what I was doing? I never knew if I was smart or not because I never really tried...but what if I did? Why not? I had nothing to lose.

## Scene Nine

---

TUAN My sponsors helped me find work. Every night and on weekends I would clean office buildings. It was hard to do that and study for school too, but I had to send money to my parents. They wanted to leave Vietnam to come and be with us. And I needed money so my sister and I could eat... Once, just before I finished work at midnight, my supervisor came around. (*mops*)

MRS. PAUL Hi, Tuan.

TUAN (*not stopping work*) Hi, Mrs. Paul.

MRS. PAUL How're you doing tonight?

TUAN (*still mopping*) Okay. Thank you.

MRS. PAUL Your sister, how's your sister?

TUAN — Sister good. Thank you.

MRS. PAUL — You're a great worker, Tuan. I wish I had five workers like you... Hey, take a break.

TUAN *does not understand, keeps mopping.*

Tuan. (*takes the mop*) Tuan, I have to tell you something. Here. (*hands* TUAN *an envelope*)

TUAN — Thank you. (*opens it*)

MRS. PAUL — Severance pay. And your separation certificate, though you don't have enough weeks to collect UIC.

TUAN — I don't understand.

MRS. PAUL — You're fired.

TUAN — I don't understand.

MRS. PAUL — No more job. You're through. No more work.

TUAN — No work?

MRS. PAUL — Right, right, you get it.

TUAN — Why no work?

MRS. PAUL — You're good son, you're one of my best men. It's nothing personal.

TUAN — Personal?

MRS. PAUL — Forget it, just forget it. It's not up to me.

TUAN Up to me?

MRS. PAUL Look, the guy who owns this building complained.

TUAN Complain?

MRS. PAUL ...look, don't make this any harder for me, kid, I already feel like a total jerk...I can't afford to lose this contract, so that's it, okay?

TUAN Work! (*takes the mop from* MRS. PAUL)

MRS. PAUL *takes the mop back.*

Why no work?

MRS. PAUL ...good luck, kid. (*exits*)

## Scene Ten

PHIROZA So for a long time I just plugged along, things were fine. I figured I could handle just about anything. And then one day...

TODD *enters, he sees* PHIROZA *who is looking at her notebook. He checks his breath, sprays with a mouth freshener. Checks his hair, sprays it too.* PHIROZA *looks. He stops, smiles sheepishly.*

TODD Hi.

PHIROZA Hi.

TODD Is your name Phiroza?

PHIROZA Yeah.

TODD I'm—Todd.

PHIROZA (*in the same breath*) —Todd.

TODD Yeah.

*Embarrassed silence.*

...you're Italian, right?

PHIROZA Maybe.

TODD Greek?

PHIROZA No.

TODD Portuguese?

PHIROZA Try again. (*to audience*) So how long could I keep up this guessing game? I liked him, I wanted him to like me. So then I did something really dumb. At the time I thought it was sort of funny. But it wasn't.

TODD Spanish?

PHIROZA No. Ready?

TODD Yeah.

PHIROZA My family comes from Persia.

TODD Persia? Far out.

PHIROZA (*to audience*) It's not a total lie. Our people did come from Persia...800 years ago.

TODD You're really from Persia?

PHIROZA Yeah, my whole family.

TODD Wow.

PHIROZA (*to audience*) We got along great. And if anyone ever gave us a rough time—

*A party horn honks.*

TODD She's from Persia, ya goof.

*Horn.*

Take your own advice, eh?

*Horn.*

PHIROZA Hey, why don't you grow up?

*Another horn.* PHIROZA *and* TODD *just smile at each other, ignoring the taunt. They kiss.*

(*to audience*) So I didn't tell him the truth.

TODD Okay, see you later.

PHIROZA Bye. (*to audience*) Not then, anyway. I didn't want to tell him until I got to know him better. I thought it was an excellent tactic—for a while.

## Scene Eleven

JENNIFER Mr. Lizard?

MR. LIZARD Yes, Miss Malcolm?

JENNIFER I'm thinking—

MR. LIZARD Thinking? Thinking, Miss Malcolm, Bravo!

JENNIFER I'm thinking about transferring into a level five programme.

MR. LIZARD Pardon me?

JENNIFER I want to get out of vocational school.

*Pause.*

MR. LIZARD Are you on drugs, Miss Malcolm?

JENNIFER I don't use drugs, Sir.

MR. LIZARD What, then, is responsible for this peculiar delusion?

JENNIFER Nothing, Sir. It isn't a delusion.

MR. LIZARD I've seen your test scores. And you are barely passing your courses at this level. How do you expect to make it in a collegiate?

JENNIFER By working harder.

MR. LIZARD There is a large difference, Miss Malcolm, between hard work and having what it takes.

JENNIFER Are you saying I don't have what it takes?

MR. LIZARD Frankly, no. You do not.

JENNIFER Well I think I do. (*to audience*) So I started working my butt off. It wasn't easy, but my grades started going up.

DELACY Hey, Jennifer, wanna go to a movie?

JENNIFER Not tonight, Delacy.

DELACY All you ever do is study.

JENNIFER I've got a test on Monday.

DELACY I thought you were lazy.

JENNIFER Okay, okay, so you were right.

DELACY You just had to learn not to believe what they said about you.

JENNIFER That I was lazy?

DELACY Because you were black.

JENNIFER Oh come on, Delacy. This is Canada, everybody's the same here. This isn't Alabama or South Africa or England.

DELACY You really think so?

JENNIFER Yeah.

DELACY What about when people call you names in the street?

JENNIFER I just ignore them.

DELACY What about when people stare at you?

JENNIFER — It's no big deal.

DELACY — And the stuff we both went through at school—everybody just assumes you're lazy and no good—you think every white person in this country goes through that too?

JENNIFER — I don't know.

DELACY — Well, you're gonna, Jennifer. Whether you like it or not.

JENNIFER — Delacy—

DELACY *exits.*

## Scene Twelve

TUAN — I had so little English, I didn't know what my supervisor was saying. But I knew what she meant. Now I know what she did was illegal. But when it happened I was upset, it didn't make sense. I needed to talk to someone.

LO *enters. He grabs the separation certificate.*

LO — Keui mm iyu nay mieh la? [What the hell is this?]

TUAN — Mo gong jo lo. [She fired me.]

LO — She fired you?

TUAN — Yeah, she fired me.

LO — Who cares, it was a stupid job anyway.

TUAN — Thanks, Lo, that makes me feel a lot better.

LO — I'm sure they liked how the work got done. They just didn't like who was doing it.

TUAN — They liked me. I know she liked me.

LO — Not enough to keep someone like us on the job. And you can't speak enough english to fight back so you're easy to mess around.

TUAN — I'll find another job, it's no big deal.

LO — What? Mopping floors?

TUAN — I don't mind it.

LO — Yeah, you're a real survivor.

TUAN — Aren't you?

LO — Maybe, but I don't mop floors. I'm a mechanic.

TUAN — You'll be okay. You'll get a job.

LO — Oh, sure, everytime I apply for one, they say: You don't have Canadian experience. How am I supposed to get experience if nobody'll hire me? Or they say: Sorry, you don't speak enough english. But how often does a mechanic have to speak to a carburetor? Besides, most of the cars here are Japanese. I speak a little Japanese. If they need somebody to talk to a Toyota, I can do it.

TUAN (*to audience*) But I knew Lo was in despair, he needed work so badly. Looking at it now, I think he was more upset about my bad fortune than even I was. Because in spite of everything, I still had hope. I had to earn money, so I didn't stop looking until I found another job. It wasn't much, but at least we could survive.

## Scene Thirteen

*A tough masked figure, as in scene six, emerges. He goes to* PHIROZA*'s locker and scribbles on it.*

*As he exits, he shoves* TUAN.

## Scene Fourteen

TODD Hey, Phiroza, get your stuff out of your locker and let's go.

PHIROZA Just a second, Todd, just a sec...oh no. (*stands in front of her locker, hiding the slur*)

TODD What is it? C'mon, let me see.

PHIROZA *moves away.* TODD *stares at the markings.*

The jerks.

PHIROZA Doesn't surprise me.

TODD Do you know who wrote this?

PHIROZA I think so.

TODD Tell me. I'll kill the goofs.

PHIROZA Perfect. You kill them, then their friends kill you. Then your friends kill their friends and then their friends' friends kill your friends and then your friends' friends kill their friends' friends and their friends' friends' friends kill—

TODD All right, all right. So what do you think we should do?

PHIROZA I guess I'll move my locker.

TODD Why should you have to do that? Put the same thing on their locker.

PHIROZA Forget it. Why spread the pollution?

TODD So you're just gonna let it happen?

PHIROZA No, I could try talking to them.

TODD Who?

PHIROZA The guys who share the locker next to mine.

TODD Oh, come on, they won't talk to you.

PHIROZA Yeah, but I wonder what would happen. You know what the big one looks like? He walks like this: (*plays both the jock and herself*) ...he's got this thing with his shoulders and this kind of strut like he's the toughest dude in the world.

JOCK — Hey boys, look at this: (*flexes his muscles*) Not bad, eh? I been working out with the Nautilus. Hey, check out that chick. Watch this, boys: Hey, baby, what's happening? Wanna watch me drink a six pack? Two six packs? Hey come back, I love you.

PHIROZA — So then I say to him: Hey, why'd you do that to my locker?

JOCK — What do you want?

PHIROZA — I want to know why you did that.

JOCK — I don't know what you're talking about.

PHIROZA — You do too. Now explain.

JOCK — I got nothin' to explain.

PHIROZA — You did it, now explain it.

JOCK — You want an explanation? It was something to do.

PHIROZA — Listen, if we would just learn to treat each other decently, we would be so much further ahead...just because I was born in— (*stops suddenly*)

TODD — Go on, great, tell him where you were born.

*She looks at* TODD.

Go on, tell him where you were born— Phiroza? What is it?

PHIROZA — Nothing. Nothing!

TODD *shrugs and exits.*

It was great, perfect. He thought I was mad at him but I was really mad at myself for that stupid lie. I liked Todd a lot, wanted him to know who I was, who I really was. But instead I was covering up all the time, faking it. I couldn't believe I was doing this to him. Or myself.

## Scene Fifteen

TUAN Sometimes late at night when I am mopping floors, I stop and listen. The empty building, so hollow. Buzzing of fluorescent tubes. Outside rain beats against windows. I feel... like I'm underwater. I think: around the corner, my older brother will be standing. Waiting to grab the mop from my hands, shouting, "You're my little brother, why are you working when you should be sleeping? Give that mop to me, that is my job!" And I look at him, and his hair is still wet, wet like it was the last time I saw him. I want to say, "Did you swim, I thought you drowned. How did you find me here, in Canada, in this city, in this building right now? You didn't drown, you're alive and you made it all the way to me."

...and I walk down the corridor, turn the corner and look. The hallway goes on forever. It's so empty. No sound but the hum of lights. And the rain against the windows.

## Scene Sixteen

*The following is performed as a mask mime narrated by* JENNIFER. *The* SHOPKEEPER, COP *and* GIRL *are white mask figures.*

JENNIFER — I was in this store near school, looking at some magazines and this girl walked in. I saw her take some stuff: earrings, a bracelet, some hair clips. She shoved it in her purse and went for the door. Just then the shopkeeper yells, "Stop!" The girl starts running but it was the shopkeeper's lucky day: a policeman was just walking in. He takes her to the counter and dumps out her purse. Out comes the earrings and bracelets and hair clips. He then tells the girl to apologize to the shopkeeper and she does. The shopkeeper accepts her apology. The girl says goodbye and leaves. Then...

*The masked figures speak. Their smiling faces turn to frowns.*

SHOPKEEPER — Wait. Don't let that girl go. I think she took something too.

JENNIFER — I was just standing here.

SHOPKEEPER — Every time those people come in here they walk out with half the stuff on my shelves.

COP — Open up your purse.

JENNIFER — But I was—

COP — Open it up!

JENNIFER See, I don't have anything.

COP Don't get cheeky with me. You people are always mouthing off. You may not be in trouble now, but you will eventually. And when you are, I'll have you behind bars so fast you won't know what hit you.

JENNIFER I want your number. I'm gonna report you.

COP Try it. You want to see harassment? Just cross the line once, baby, and you'll get it. I know how to deal with your kind.

*The mask figures freeze, staring at the audience.*

JENNIFER (*to audience*) This is Canada. In 1988. but it happened, it really happened. I know most police aren't like that guy. But some are. And how many people are too? I started thinking about all the times I've been bugged in stores— Can I help you? Can I help you? They all thought I was shoplifting. And the time our neighbors asked us a million questions about how we were able to afford our new car. I wonder if they thought we stole it? And walking down the street, the names little four and five year olds have called me—where did they learn that stuff? I didn't teach it to them. Who did?

## Scene Seventeen

| | |
|---|---|
| TUAN | My sister always says that I work too hard, mopping floors or going to school. She wants to help earn money but I won't let her. She's too young and I promised my parents I'd take care of her. Besides, at least I had work. |
| LO | Wai! A-Dwon! [Hey, Tuan!] |
| TUAN | Gum yeh, nay hoy been doe a? [It's late, why are you here?] Lo, it's late. What are you doing here? |
| LO | Going home. |
| TUAN | Good, we can walk together. |
| LO | Not that home. |
| TUAN | What do you mean? |
| LO | I'm going back to Vietnam. |
| TUAN | Going back? After all you went through to come to Canada? |
| LO | I thought it would be different. |
| TUAN | It is different, it's free. |
| LO | You call this free? Look at this. |
| TUAN | A letter. From your parents...they seem to be very impressed with you. |

LO — And proud and happy. I spend all day looking for jobs when there aren't any and they think I'm a big success in Canada, making tons of money fixing monorail trains.

TUAN — You don't fix monorail trains.

LO — Don't tell them that. They're all ready to fly here to live in my five bedroom house as soon as I send them their plane tickets.

TUAN — You told them you have a five bedroom house?

LO — My room here is worse than anything I ever had in Vietnam... Tuan—I'm going home.

TUAN — You can't go back to Vietnam.

LO — So?

TUAN — Maybe you need a holiday.

LO — What, take a cruise on the Love Boat?

TUAN — Well, no, go to Niagara Falls or something.

LO — That's a good idea.

TUAN — I can lend you some money.

LO — I've got enough.

TUAN — Great. Let's get something to eat.

LO — Not right now. I've got a lot to do to get ready.

TUAN — Okay.

LO ...thanks for everything Tuan. Daw jeh sai nay la. [Thank you for everything.] You've been a good friend. (*starts to exit*)

TUAN (*stops him*) Wai. Nay yow mu see-ah? [Hey, what's going on?]

LO Mo see. [Nothing.]

LO *exits.*

TUAN We spoke the same language but I didn't understand what he was saying. If I really knew I would have held onto him, not let him walk off alone. I would have run to his room, locked his windows...but I didn't understand and I let him walk away...let him die. His apartment building was too tall. The lights in the city shimmer so much at night they're like light on the water. It all looks so soft and inviting. He must have floated like a leaf in the wind just above the waves. Then one drop of water touches it and it never leaves the sea again. But it wasn't water, it was the sidewalk. And he was not a leaf.

## Scene Eighteen

MR. LIZARD Well, Miss Malcolm, you did it. You're transferring into a collegiate. Congratulations.

JENNIFER Thank you, Sir.

MR. LIZARD I always knew you could do it.

JENNIFER — Pardon me?

MR. LIZARD — I always knew you had it in you.

JENNIFER — You did?

MR. LIZARD — I only pushed you because I could see your potential. I could see that little spark of intelligence still glowing. I nurtured it, I made it grow. And here you are. Congratulations.

JENNIFER — Don't congratulate me. You say you act tough to help us out but all you do is make us feel stupid and worthless. Cause you do, you do think we're stupid. You never thought I could do it, you never did. All you did was make me feel like a fool but I made it anyway, in spite of you. So, Mr. Lizard, I have just one thing to say to you: OUT. YOU. GO!!

*Music: Bob Marley's "I Shot The Sheriff."*

## Scene Nineteen

PHIROZA — So Todd kept thinking I was from Persia. But I was really sick of the lie. I had to be so careful about everything I said to him. I wanted him to meet my family—but what if he started asking my dad questions about life in Persia? I decided to tell him the truth —but it wasn't going to be easy.

TODD — Hey, Phiroza, where'd you put my Springsteen tape?

PHIROZA *hands him a card.*

Thanks. What's this? A birth certificate? It's yours. Place of birth: Bombay, India. ...I thought you were from Persia.

PHIROZA That's right, we're from Persia.

TODD Then why does it say India?

PHIROZA Because I grew up in India.

TODD It says you were born in India.

PHIROZA I lived in India till I was four.

TODD And then you went back to Persia to be born?

PHIROZA No, then I went to Canada.

TODD I thought you said you were from Persia.

PHIROZA I am.

TODD So did you get born twice, once in Persia and once in India?

PHIROZA No.

TODD Let me see if I've got it. You were born in India, then you came to Canada but you're from Persia.

PHIROZA You've got it.

TODD I do? Ever been to Persia?

PHIROZA Personally?

TODD — Yes, personally.

PHIROZA — I was one of the Parsi people who came from Persia to India.

TODD — When?

PHIROZA — When?

TODD — Yeah, when.

PHIROZA — Oh, about...eight (*mumbles*) years ago.

TODD — Eight years ago?

PHIROZA — Not exactly.

TODD — Eight how many years ago.

PHIROZA — Hundred.

TODD — Eight hundred years ago? You went from Persia eight hundred years ago and came to India and were born and came to Canada when you were four?

PHIROZA — Because I was born again, like reincarnation.

TODD — I think you're the first older woman I ever went out with.

PHIROZA — I'm the same age as you.

TODD — Right. I see. You were born in this life, so this is the life that counts, right?

PHIROZA — Right.

TODD — So in this life, you were born in India, right?

PHIROZA ...right.

TODD And in this life, you're Canadian, right?

PHIROZA ...right.

TODD ...right. So that makes you...

PHIROZA ...Indo-Canadian.

TODD Right.

PHIROZA Right...sorry for putting you on for so long. I should have told you sooner but the longer I waited, the harder it got to tell you, and I didn't know what to say...sorry. (*slight pause*) Do you want to break up?

TODD Nah.

PHIROZA For sure?

TODD Yeah...cause I have a confession to make too.

PHIROZA You do?

TODD Yeah.

PHIROZA What is it?

TODD Well...you know I told you I was in Grade Twelve, supposed to graduate this year—

PHIROZA What grade are you in!

TODD I was afraid to tell you—

PHIROZA What grade!

TODD ...Three.

PHIROZA What? How old are you?

TODD Seven. You wanna break up?

PHIROZA Get out of here!

TODD I am, I'm seven years old. These are new teeth, see?

PHIROZA You nut!

TODD You wanna break up?

PHIROZA No, I like younger men.

TODD Oh, whew!

PHIROZA You like older women?

TODD Oh yeah.

PHIROZA Whew! (*to audience*) Hey, that wasn't so bad. I could have told him the first day we met. I guess I knew from the start how he felt about me. I just wasn't sure how I felt about myself.

## Scene Twenty

---

JENNIFER Sometimes I wonder—was Mr. Lizard telling the truth? Did he treat me that way on purpose? Or was he what I thought he was? He did treat Delacy the same way. I guess it's like everything else in this country—hard to see.

I'm in a collegiate now, and I'm doing okay, even if it is a lot of work. Sometimes I see the kids from my old school and they give me a hard time—but the ones who are my real friends understand, they're behind me. So I think I'm going to go to university. Maybe I'll train to be a teacher. Or a lawyer. I don't know, I haven't decided yet. But I will.

TUAN When I found out Lo was dead, it was such a puzzle. Why should I live and Lo die? We were so much the same—why not me? I remember he always said that I was a survivor. He'd laugh, tease me...now, I just wish he was a survivor too. By next year I will have enough money to bring my parents here. I'm glad they will be safe. They are very excited, but as for me, I don't want to think about the future. For me, it is as hard to look forward as it is to look back. So I live for today. For each moment. And live as best I can.

PHIROZA My name is Phiroza Mehta. I was born in—(*looks at* TODD) —Bombay, India.

JENNIFER My name is Jennifer Malcolm. I was born in Toronto, Ontario.

TUAN My name is Wong Tuan Hung. I was born in Hanoi, North Vietnam.

PHIROZA I have two arms.

JENNIFER Two legs.

TUAN Two eyes.

PHIROZA I feel

JENNIFER I feel

TUAN I feel

ALL I feel.

*The End.*

# LIARS

*Liars* was first produced by Green Thumb Theatre on tour in British Columbia in the Fall of 1986, with the following cast:

| | |
|---|---|
| LENNY | *Karin Konoval* |
| JACE | *Allan Zinyk* |
| *Lenny's* MOTHER; TEACHER | *Barbara Russell* |
| *Lenny's* DAD; *Jace's* FATHER | *Kevin McNulty* |

*Directed by Keith Turnbull.*
*Designed by Marti Wright.*
*Stage Managed by Michael Cunningham.*

The Characters

LENNY: *A 16 year old girl. She is very well groomed and dresses fashionably conservative.*

JACE: *A 16 year old boy. He is on the fringes of the headbanger crowd. Blue jeans, black leather jacket and a Jimi Hendrix T-shirt.*

TEACHER
MOTHER, *Lenny's*
DAD, *Lenny's*
FATHER, *Jace's*

## Staging Note

*In the original production, life-sized dummies were used to portray the parents' alcoholism. The dummies' faces and shapes resembled the actors, and each was dressed in the same clothes. Not only were the dummies used as protectors and playmates for the parents, but in the case of Jace's* FATHER*'s a weapon, with which to smash* JACE *to the ground.*

*Each dummy should always be present with the respective parent, but not to the degree that it becomes distracting to the audience or a problem for the actor.*

*I have indicated some key places where the use of the dummies is particularly important.*

## The Set

*The play takes place in a wide variety of locales, and these are established through the dialogue. The set should be a flexible, neutral area.*

## AUTHOR'S NOTE

*I would like to thank a number of people for their time, advice and support: Durb Stenback, a counselor specializing in Adult Children of Alcoholics' issues; Kathleen Wood, Juanita Arthur, Terry Kyle and the original cast and director, who gave so much of their time and ideas to the script.*

*Particular thanks are due to Laura Westlake and Loanne Anderson of the Burnaby Alcohol and Drug Program, and the participants of their Youth Drug Information Workshop. The kids in the workshop allowed me to take part as a member, and shared their time and feelings generously. It is to them, and their struggle that I dedicate this play.*

## Scene One

*Classroom.*

JACE *and* LENNY. LENNY sits attentively. JACE *has feet up, staring at ceiling.*

TEACHER (*voice over*) Sister Cities. A kind of partnership between cities. Shared activities. Jason, name a shared activity.

JACE Sex.

TEACHER Between cities?

JACE Where there's a will there's a way.

TEACHER Please sit up and pay attention. Leonore, activities.

LENNY Trade, culture, education.

JACE Drugs.

TEACHER Jason, that was uncalled for.

JACE It's true. Dope is a big activity. Big business. Between cities.

TEACHER Young man, if you think you are so clever, why don't you name for us, right now, Vancouver's Sister Cities.

JACE Sure.

TEACHER Well?

JACE There's uh...

LENNY (*whispers to* JACE) Yokohama.

JACE What?

LENNY Yokohama!

TEACHER Speak up.

JACE Yoko Ono.

LENNY Yokohama!

TEACHER Jason?

JACE I said it. Yoko Ono.

TEACHER Yokohama. A city in Japan. Not Yoko Ono.

JACE Sorry. Bad pronunciation.

TEACHER Leonore, what can you tell us about Yokohama?

LENNY Well, in the eleventh century—

JACE Give me a break.

LENNY —what's now Yokohama was ruled by Samurai warriors.

JACE Samurai? (*doing a Samurai swordsman*) Hiii Yaa!

TEACHER Jace.

JACE *does a Samurai apology.*

Go on, Leonore.

LENNY — The thing was, Japan was completely closed to the world for centuries, it was totally isolated.

JACE — (*bored*) Incredible.

LENNY — Then, in 1853, Admiral Perry came to Yokohama with his "black fleet" and Japan was opened to the rest of the world.

JACE — (*excited*) Oh, wow! (*instantly asleep, snoring loudly*)

TEACHER — Jace!

JACE — Yes, honorable teacher?

TEACHER — Just what do you think you are doing?

JACE — Good question.

TEACHER — What's a good question?

JACE — Just what *are* we doing here?

TEACHER — Get out.

JACE — My pleasure, honorable teacher.

JACE *does another flurry of Samurai sword strokes, suddenly stops, bows to* TEACHER, *and exits.*

*Music.*

LENNY *exits.*

## Scene Two

*Lunchroom.*

LENNY *sits down, starts eating her lunch.* JACE *enters, sits down next to her.*

JACE Hi.

LENNY *keeps eating her lunch.*

Hi.

JACE *bends around, sticking his face nose to nose with hers.*

Hi.

LENNY *is silent. Pause.*

That's some lunch you got there. Hey, that's real bread on your sandwich. That is not a chemical substitute. Did you make that bread?

LENNY *very slightly nods yes.*

You know, I've never eaten homemade bread. Is it really good for you?

LENNY *hands him half a sandwich.*

Hey, there's lettuce in this sandwich. A tomato. Gross! What's this white stuff?

LENNY Cheese.

JACE — Cheese. Yuk. I don't touch the stuff. I like bugs. Beetles, ants, slugs. Health food. (*tastes it*) Hm. Not bad. Sure beats Velveeta. You could probably grow up big and strong eating this stuff. Thanks. I had a terrible case of the munchies.

LENNY — Are you stoned?

JACE — It's a way to survive in this boring and useless prison.

LENNY — You mean school?

JACE — Exactly.

LENNY — I could never go to school high.

JACE — You should try it sometime. You might learn something. So who makes you the fancy sandwiches? Mommy?

LENNY — No.

JACE — Don't tell me it's Daddy.

LENNY — No.

JACE — Then who? You got a housekeeper?

LENNY — Sort of. Yeah.

JACE — Maid service. Some people have all the luck.

LENNY — Yeah.

JACE — Hey, listen, uh—sorry for giving you a hard time in there. It's just when you mentioned Japan, I got Samurai Fever. Hiiiiya!

LENNY I should have kept my mouth shut.

JACE It's all right, I just don't see the point.

LENNY You don't know. You don't know a thing about those cities.

JACE Who cares?

LENNY You should. They're beautiful. They're different. Nothing's the same as it is here. It's another world.

JACE (*grinning*) I go to other worlds all the time.

LENNY It's not the same. When I start travelling, I'm really going to go. And I'm not coming back.

JACE What?

LENNY Forget it.

JACE Hey, Lenny—

LENNY What did you call me?

JACE Lenny. Leonore sucks. What're you doing Saturday night?

LENNY I don't know.

JACE I'll pick you up at seven.

LENNY What?

JACE *exits.*

*Music.*

## Scene Three

LENNY*'s house.*

MOTHER*'s theme music. (perhaps from Madame Butterfly)*

MOTHER *enters. She is singing with the aria, holding a lifesized dummy of herself, and drinking from a champagne glass.*

*She and the dummy fall to the ground.* LENNY *enters.*

LENNY — Hi, I'm home! Anybody here? (*looks around; spots* MOTHER) Mom. Mom, are you okay?

MOTHER — Hi, baby.

LENNY — I'll help you up. Come on, I'll help you up.

MOTHER — Oh you always help me. You're such a good girl.

LENNY *struggles to get* MOTHER , *who holds the dummy, back in chair. Finally she manages to seat her. Then she starts picking up empty bottles.*

LENNY — Don't worry, I'm cleaning up. Everything'll be fine.

*She starts sweeping and tidying. The phone rings.*

Coming.

MOTHER *and dummy fall off chair.* LENNY *tries to pick* MOTHER *up.*

Come on, Mom, please. The phone.

*She puts* MOTHER *back on chair. Grabs phone.*

Hello?

MOTHER *starts to fall over.* LENNY *holds her up as she talks.*

DAD Hello, Leonore? Are you all right?

LENNY Yeah, right, everything's fine. Hi, Dad.

DAD Listen, kid, I'm sorry but I'm tied up in a meeting. I'll be late for dinner.

LENNY That's all right.

DAD What're you making?

LENNY Your favorite. Beef Stroganoff.

DAD Great. Tell you what, I'll bring back some corn on the cob on the way home.

LENNY That'd be good, Dad.

DAD And thanks for that great lunch. What kind of cheese was that anyway?

LENNY Gouda.

DAD Your sandwiches are the best. How's Mom?

LENNY She's okay.

DAD Can I talk to her?

LENNY I don't think so.

DAD Is something wrong?

LENNY The usual.

DAD Oh. Did anyone see her?

LENNY I don't think so. I found her inside.

DAD Good. Did you get a chance to iron those shirts for me?

LENNY I'm going to do them as soon as I finish the vacuuming.

DAD Great honey, thanks. You're an angel. See you around eight.

LENNY Okay. Dad...

DAD Yes, darling?

LENNY ...nothing. See you.

DAD Bye.

LENNY *hangs up the phone. She then helps her* MOTHER *off.*

MOTHER I love you so much, Sweetheart. My little girl.

*Music.*

## Scene Four

*JACE's house.*

*FATHER's theme music. (perhaps Charlie Pride's "Kiss An Angel Good Morning")*

*FATHER enters with dummy of himself, dancing and singing along with the music. He sits, picks up a small television set, starts fiddling with the back of it.*

*JACE enters.*

JACE — Yoo hoo! Anybody home? Hi, Dad, how're ya doing?

FATHER — What'd you do with the screwdriver?

JACE — Nothing. I didn't see it.

FATHER — I'm fixing the TV set. Get me the screwdriver.

JACE — Did you look in the toolbox?

FATHER — Of course I looked in the toolbox, you idiot. Where else would I look?

JACE — I don't know.

FATHER — Where'd you put it!

JACE — What're you asking me for, I didn't touch it.

FATHER — Get me that screwdriver and my beer right now.

JACE All right, all right.

*JACE comes back with the screwdriver and beer.*

FATHER All right, that's my kid. Good work, boy. Two things a guy's gotta have. His beer and his screwdriver. Aren't you gonna have one?

JACE Not right now.

FATHER What's with you Jace, won't have a beer with the old man?

JACE Okay.

FATHER Atta boy. You're a good kid, Jace. You're all right. You found my screwdriver. Where was it?

JACE In the toolbox.

FATHER Right where I said it would be. Didn't I? Didn't I tell you where it was?

JACE It was right where you said it would be...Dad—

FATHER Yeah, what is it, I'm all ears.

JACE I wanna ask a favor...

FATHER Sure, what is it, son—you name it.

JACE Can I have the car Saturday night?

FATHER The car? You wanna borrow the car? Saturday night?

JACE Yeah.

FATHER No problem. It's all yours. I'm not using it. What's mine is yours, kid.

JACE Thanks.

FATHER You're very welcome. So what are you up to?

JACE Gotta date.

FATHER Oh yeah? Somebody new?

JACE Yeah. Her name's Leonore. But I call her Lenny.

FATHER Hey, I think you like this girl.

JACE She's all right.

FATHER Just like your old man, playing it cool—but I bet you got goosebumps lining your stomach.

*They both laugh.*

JACE You think she knows I'm nervous?

FATHER Doesn't matter, she'll like you for who you are.

JACE I guess so.

FATHER No sweat.

JACE All right.

*They slap hands. Pause.* FATHER *takes a long drink of his beer, then crushes the can.*

FATHER Where's my screwdriver?

JACE ...you just had it.

FATHER What are you talking about? Where is it?

JACE It was right there.

FATHER Don't give me that crap, where'd you put it?

JACE Here it is.

FATHER You're always losing my stuff. That time you took my razor.

JACE I was five years old.

FATHER You steal my stuff.

JACE I didn't know what I was doing.

FATHER You never know what you're doing. How're you gonna make it in this world if you don't take responsibility!

JACE I was five.

FATHER How'm I supposed to shave without my razor? Get your own damn razor!

JACE I've got my own razor, I don't need yours.

FATHER You just stay outta my stuff. I don't do enough for you, you take everything? I looked all over the house for that damn razor. I was late for the interview. I didn't get the job. How'm I supposed to get work if everybody's always losing my stuff?

JACE — I didn't do anything.

FATHER — Get outta here. Get out! (*shoves* JACE)

JACE — You stupid drunk.

FATHER — What'd you call me?

JACE — You heard me.

FATHER — Come here and say it to me.

*Pause.* JACE *exits.*

Where's my screwdriver!

*Music.*

## Scene Five

*Outside school.*

*From one side of the stage,* LENNY *enters.*

*From the other side, a Japanese mask figure in kimono enters, holding a tray with teapot and two cups. The figure might resemble a kokeshi doll.*

LENNY *and the figure meet in the centre, kneel and begin a stylized version of a tea ceremony. Their movements are very formal, precise.*

JACE *enters.*

*The music fades out.*

*The figure gathers up the pot and cups, and places a pen and paper in* LENNY*'s hand.* LENNY *begins writing.*

JACE What are you writing?

LENNY A letter.

*The figure exits.*

JACE To who?

LENNY Nobody.

JACE *grabs the letter. Reads.*

JACE Dear Et...Etsk...

LENNY Etsuko.

JACE Edsuckhole... Thank you for your letter. (*to* LENNY) What is she, a pen pal?

LENNY That's right.

JACE (*reading*) I would love to experience a tea ceremony with you. (*to* LENNY) What else do you want to experience with her?

LENNY Lay off.

JACE (*reading*) I would love to live in Japan forever. (*to* LENNY) Why do you want to escape to Japan?

LENNY None of your business.

JACE You're absolutely right, it's none of my business. Why do you wanna take off? Something wrong? Too much pressure at school, didn't get an A plus plus on the last cheerleading exam? Oh, then it must be at home—oh, don't tell me, did your maid die? It's so hard finding good help these days.

LENNY You don't understand.

JACE No, I wouldn't. You've got it so perfect. You should just see what I have to live with. It's 100 percent pure insanity and death.

LENNY Why?

JACE My dad's a drunk.

LENNY What?

JACE You heard me.

LENNY That's a pretty harsh thing to say.

JACE It's true.

LENNY But he could just be having a hard time right now. Psychological problems.

JACE You're not kidding.

LENNY See? He probably just needs your support.

JACE Sure, cause he can't stand up.

LENNY C'mon.

JACE How would you know? You've never seen him. He calls himself my father but he doesn't even know how old I am. Whenever I go home I don't know whether he'll be laughing it up or passed out on the floor drowning in a pool of his own puke. Ever picked up your father and cleaned him off and have him look at you and not know who you are? (*pause*) Sorry, I didn't mean to shock you.

LENNY You didn't shock me, it's...I know somebody just like that.

JACE You do? Who?

LENNY A friend of mine... Tracy. She's really...got a lot of problems. A lot of responsibility.

JACE Maybe she should just split.

LENNY She can't. She's got to take care of things. Her mom needs a lot of help.

JACE Oh, cause her old lady's a drunk.

LENNY I don't think so. I don't know.

JACE Have you seen her?

LENNY Yeah.

JACE And you can't tell?

LENNY We thought she was just depressed.

JACE I'm sure she is. Especially when she's sober. You should introduce me to your friend. Maybe I could talk to her.

LENNY She lives outside of town.

JACE Well, listen, I have the car Saturday night. We could go visit her.

LENNY I don't think so. She's really shy. And if anybody found out she was talking about this stuff, she'd get in big trouble.

JACE So I guess if she knew you talked to me—she'd be pretty upset.

LENNY For sure.

JACE Okay, look, it's just between us then.

LENNY Good.

JACE Hey, I think you're pretty hot.

LENNY Yeah?

JACE Really.

LENNY Sure.

JACE Don't you know how to accept a compliment?

LENNY Yeah.

JACE What do you say?

LENNY Thank you.

JACE You're welcome.

*Music.*

## Scene Six

LENNY*'s house.* DAD *is behind a newspaper.*

LENNY Dad?

DAD Yes, Sweetie?

LENNY Can I talk to you?

DAD Sure, honey, what is it?

LENNY I want to talk about Mom.

DAD Why?

LENNY I'm worried about her. I think she needs help.

DAD We're all giving her help, sweetheart.

LENNY But she's getting worse.

DAD It doesn't seem that way to me.

LENNY That's because you're never home.

DAD Now is that a fair thing to say?

LENNY You don't see her like I do.

DAD Of course I see your mother. I know how she's suffering. Her life has been filled with tragedy.

LENNY I know, Dad. But I think she needs help.

DAD — Look, it's hard for both of us, Leonore, but we have to keep this boat afloat. I am under amazing pressure at work—I am building an office tower. Two hundred men are trusting me with their lives. I can't afford to be weak or confused for one second. Could you imagine what would happen if I lost their confidence?

LENNY — The building would fall down.

DAD — Total destruction. Total chaos. We have to be strong. We have to protect your mother.

LENNY — But what if she's an alcoholic?

DAD — Pardon me?

LENNY — If she's an alcoholic, she needs help.

*Pause.*

DAD — Leonore. Any help she needs she can get inside this house. There is a huge difference between your mother's personal problems and something like that.

LENNY — I don't think there is.

DAD — Honey, please. I am under too much pressure already. Don't start making new problems for me...oh no.

LENNY — What is it, Dad?

DAD — I knew it. I'm getting a migraine.

LENNY — I'll get you one of your pills.

DAD — They're in my briefcase.

LENNY Here.

DAD No these are my tranquilizers. I need the pain killers. Ow.

LENNY Dad, are you all right?

DAD Yeah, I'll be okay, I'll be okay. My head fells like it's splitting right open.

LENNY Dad, I'm sorry.

DAD Sorry about what?

LENNY What I said—about Mom.

DAD Just forget about it. I'll pretend I never heard it.

LENNY You will?

DAD For you, I will, of course. I love you Darling. I know you want to do what's best.

LENNY Right.

DAD I'm just going to lie down for a while.

LENNY *watches* DAD *exit.*

*Music.*

## Scene Seven

*JACE's house. JACE is getting ready for his date. He smells his arm pits, grimaces. He takes off his black T-shirt and puts on an identical one.*

*Finally, after various other rituals, he is ready to go.*

JACE — Hey, Dad, I'm going now.

FATHER — Great son! Where to?

JACE — I got that date. Can I have the keys?

FATHER — A date! Deluxe. Who is she?

JACE — I told you, Lenny.

FATHER — She on birth control?

JACE — Huh?

FATHER — She on the pill or what?

JACE — How should I know?

FATHER — Well you're going out with her, aren't ya?

JACE — This is the first time we've gone out.

FATHER — You can talk to me, Son, you can tell your old man what's going on.

JACE — There's nothing happening.

FATHER — Well, be prepared or you'll knock her up and end up with something like you! (*laughs*)

JACE — Lay off, Dad.

FATHER — It's no joke. I was just like you, then one night in heaven and I'm stuck with a screaming wife and a screaming kid. Life's full of little surprises.

JACE — I'll be careful. Can I have the car keys now?

FATHER — Why?

JACE — So I can go on my date.

FATHER — What do you need the car for?

JACE — What do you think I need the car for?

FATHER — Take the bus.

JACE — You promised me the car.

FATHER — When?

JACE — Wednesday night. You said no problem you weren't using it.

FATHER — I'm not using it, my buddy Burke is.

JACE — What?

FATHER — He's moving, he needs it.

JACE — But you promised it to me.

FATHER — When?

JACE — I told you when. You promised.

FATHER — I did not. I couldn't have.

JACE Yes you did. I was there. I heard you.

FATHER Bull.

JACE You said I could have it.

FATHER I did not.

JACE You did.

FATHER Are you calling me a liar?

FATHER *picks up the dummy.*

JACE Either you're a liar or you were so drunk you blacked out.

FATHER Now you're calling me a drunk.

JACE You tell me what you are then, I don't know. You keep changing on me, I never know who the hell I'm talking to, I don't know what you want.

FATHER I'll tell you what I want: a little respect.

JACE You want some respect? Quit drinking!

FATHER Why should I?

JACE Cause you're a drunk.

FATHER What did you say?

JACE You heard me.

FATHER Come here and say that.

*Pause.* JACE *goes to him. Grabs the dummy.*

JACE — You're a drunk.

FATHER — You son of a— (*pulls the dummy out of* JACE*'s arms and hits him with it*) You want another one, say it again.

JACE *goes to him.*

JACE — You're a drunk.

FATHER *hits* JACE *with the dummy again.* JACE *goes down.* JACE *stands up and walks to him.*

You're a drunk.

FATHER *goes to hit him again. This time* JACE *pushes the dummy aside.*

I've had it with you. I'm going. I'm gone.

FATHER — You'll be back.

JACE — For what?

*Music.*

## Scene Eight

---

LENNY*'s house.* LENNY *is getting ready.*

MOTHER *enters. She holds the dummy.*

MOTHER — You look wonderful, Leonore.

LENNY — Thanks, Mom.

MOTHER Where are you going?

LENNY I don't know yet.

MOTHER A surprise date?

LENNY I guess so.

MOTHER That'll be fun. Who are you going with?

LENNY His name's Jason.

MOTHER Jason. He was a mythical hero.

LENNY Jace is pretty mythical.

MOTHER This sounds serious.

LENNY He's great, Mom. He's really different. I've never met anyone like him.

MOTHER How long has this been going on?

LENNY A week or so, I don't know.

MOTHER Why didn't you tell me?

LENNY Tell you?

MOTHER About him. Jason. The mythical hero.

LENNY I tried but—

MOTHER Did you tell your father about him? (*pause*) So you told him but you didn't tell me.

LENNY Mom, I tried.

MOTHER You never tell me anything.

LENNY — Sometimes it's really hard.

MOTHER — But it's not hard to talk to him.

LENNY — Mom—

MOTHER — You never talk to me, you're always judging me, it's not fair.

LENNY — Mom, I'm not—

MOTHER — You don't understand what I'm going through, you don't understand how hard it is. I gave up everything for that man. My career, my dreams. And then he cuts me right out of his life. He's cut me out of everything.

DAD *enters.*

If you cared about me for two seconds I wouldn't be so screwed up.

DAD — And I suppose that's my fault.

MOTHER — Give me a break! Do you hear him? Mr. Innocent!

LENNY — Mom—

MOTHER — Do you think he's ever got any time for me?

DAD — Somebody's got to support this family.

MOTHER — There's a lot more to support than the bucks, mister.

DAD — If it weren't for the bucks you wouldn't be able to sit on your fat butt all day.

MOTHER — This fat butt got you through school! This fat butt coached you through your exams and paid the bills. And what do I get for it? Nothing! I'll tell you something, honey, he may be Mr. HiRise out there, but in the sack he's a nobody.

DAD — You are an obnoxious pathetic mess.

*The doorbell rings. Pause.*

Someone's at the door.

MOTHER — Who could that be?

LENNY — Jace.

MOTHER *and* DAD *suddenly transform into charming, smiling gentility, as they hide the dummy.*

MOTHER — Do you think he'd like an hors d'oeuvre, Leonore?

LENNY — Don't worry about it.

DAD — Bring your young man in!

LENNY *brings* JASON *in.*

LENNY — Hi.

JACE — Hi.

LENNY — This is my dad. Dad, this is Jason.

DAD — Hello, Jason.

JACE — Hello, Sir.

MOTHER How do you do, Jason?

LENNY This is my mom.

MOTHER I'm sure he's figured that out.

JACE Right. Pleased to meet you.

MOTHER That's an interesting T-shirt you have on.

JACE Thanks.

MOTHER Personally, I'm a Bon Jovi fan.

JACE You are?

MOTHER I like it loud.

JACE Great.

DAD So what's the plan for tonight, Jason?

JACE Not much. It's a nice night. Thought we'd go for a walk.

MOTHER Very romantic.

LENNY Mom.

DAD Have fun, kids.

LENNY 'night Mom, 'night Dad.

MOTHER Take care.

JACE Nice to meet you.

MOTHER Bye.

*They exit.* DAD *and* MOTHER *glare at each other.*

MOTHER *picks up the dummy.*

*They exit.*

## Scene Nine

*The lake.*

LENNY — Where are we?

JACE — Never been here before?

LENNY — Feels like it's the middle of nowhere.

JACE — It's the middle of the park. Just that it's at night. The night changes things.

LENNY — Yeah.

JACE — What was that! (*sneaks off*)

LENNY — (*looks for him*) What? Jace!

*Pause.* JACE *pokes her.* LENNY *shrieks.*

JACE — Got ya!

LENNY — Don't do that!

JACE — Relax. We're in the city. The worse thing you could meet is a goose with rabies.

LENNY What's in the knapsack.

JACE My gear.

LENNY What gear?

JACE My personal belongings. The essentials. See?

JACE *reaches into the pack and pulls out four black T-shirts, one after the other.*

LENNY ...what are you doing with this stuff?

JACE I moved out today.

LENNY You left home? Why?

JACE My dad and I have philosophical differences. (*shows her the bruise*)

LENNY Are you okay?

JACE Oh yeah. I feel no pain.

LENNY What do you mean?

JACE I got a little help from my friends.

LENNY What are you on?

JACE A little of this, a little of that.

LENNY Where are you going to stay?

JACE Here. This is my new place. In fact, you're sitting in the living room.

LENNY You're really going to live outside?

JACE — The weather's nice. I'll just stash my bag in the brush, nobody'll spot me.

LENNY — What if the weather changes?

JACE — I'll cross that bridge when I come to it. It's no big deal. Your friend Tracy should do the same thing.

LENNY — No, Tracy can still talk to her parents. She's not like you. Anyways, you're crazy.

JACE — No, I'm sane. Staying there is crazy. Sooner or later one of us is gonna get killed.

LENNY — It's that bad.

JACE — I couldn't stand it anymore. He's always out of it. Never there. Killing himself and dragging me down with him. I had to get out of there... Let's play something.

LENNY — What?

JACE — Tag.

LENNY — It's too dark.

JACE — (*tagging her*) You're it!

*He runs away.* LENNY *pauses, then joins the chase. She tags him.*

LENNY — You're it!

JACE — (*chasing and tagging her*) You're it!

JACE *runs away, then hides, thinking he's safe.* LENNY *sneaks up and pokes him in the ribs.*

LENNY You're it!

JACE *shrieks. They laugh.*

JACE What do you wanna play now?

LENNY Is this what you do on dates? Play kids' games?

JACE Yeah, why not? I got it. Truth, Dare, Double Dare. Ever played it?

LENNY No, what is it?

JACE (*gleefully*) You never played it?

LENNY No.

JACE Okay, we take turns, you pick one. If you pick Truth, you have to answer any question I ask and you have to be honest. If you pick Dare, you have to do whatever I say.

LENNY I don't think I like this game.

JACE Don't worry, no weird stuff, okay? If you pick Double Dare it's not as outrageous as Dare, but you have to do it twice. What do you say?

LENNY I don't know.

JACE Come on, it won't kill you. You start. Truth, Dare, Double Dare.

LENNY What?

JACE Pick one.

LENNY Pick one?

JACE Truth, Dare, Double Dare.

LENNY Double Dare.

JACE Okay. I double dare you to yell, "I've got runny zits."

LENNY What!

JACE As loud as you can. Twice.

LENNY You're kidding.

JACE Come on. Do it!

LENNY I've got runny zits!

JACE Again. Louder.

LENNY (*yells*) I've got runny zits!

JACE Don't tell me your problems. Okay, now it's my turn.

LENNY Truth, Dare, Double Dare.

JACE Dare.

LENNY ...I can't think of one.

JACE Dare me to take off my clothes.

LENNY No way! Swim across the lake and back.

JACE I can't.

LENNY I did it. Now it's your turn.

JACE — But I can't swim. Well, I guess you have to punish me.

LENNY — Punish you?

JACE — The punishment is you have to spank me.

LENNY — What?

JACE — Those are the rules. Don't blame me, I didn't make them up.

LENNY — Then who did?

JACE — Mr. Rogers.

LENNY — I'm not going to spank you.

JACE — Sorry, you have to. The rules.

LENNY — No!

JACE *lays across her legs.*

JACE — Spank!

LENNY *lightly spanks him once. He gets up.*

Now it's your turn. Truth, Dare, Double Dare?

LENNY — Dare.

JACE — Swim across the lake.

LENNY — I'm not swimming across the lake.

JACE — Punishment.

LENNY No!

JACE Mr. Rogers'll come and chop you up in little pieces!

LENNY Okay, okay.

*She lies across his legs. He lightly spanks her once.*

Truth, Dare, Double Dare.

JACE Truth.

LENNY Why did your dad hit you?

JACE He said I could have the car, but he forgot, as always. I got mad, we got into a fight. He hit me... Truth, Dare, Double Dare.

LENNY Truth.

JACE Are you Tracy?

LENNY What?

JACE Your friend Tracy is really you. True?

*Pause.*

LENNY How did you know?

JACE You think just cause I'm stoned I don't know what's going on?

LENNY When you were outside the house...before you rang the bell...

JACE
I could've used earplugs. And I could smell your mom a mile away... I have to admit, I had you figured all wrong. I thought you were Miss Preppie Universe, but you're really just a different version of a screwed up mess like me.

LENNY
That's not true.

JACE
Maybe not for Leonore but it is for Tracy.

LENNY
You and I are completely different. My dad doesn't beat me up. I don't have to run away from home. My dad works really hard to keep things together and I do too. We have to keep working, we have to keep trying no matter how hard it gets because then... because then...

JACE
...then what?

LENNY
She'll get better. If we do it right maybe she'll get better.

*Pause.*

Sometimes I think I'll come home and it *will* be all better. I walk in the house one day and everything's...

MOTHER *enters.*

MOTHER
Hi Lenny, you're home.

LENNY
Hi, Mom.

MOTHER
How was school?

LENNY
Oh, so-so, I got a **B** on the Socials exam.

| | |
|---|---|
| MOTHER | So why the long face, that's a fine grade. |
| LENNY | I know you and Dad expect better. |
| MOTHER | We just want you to do the best you can. And I know you do, so don't worry about it. |
| LENNY | ...thanks. I'd better get dinner started. |
| MOTHER | It's in the oven. Beef Stroganoff. Your favorite. |
| LENNY | Really? |
| MOTHER | You think you're the only cook in the family? |
| LENNY | No, I— |
| MOTHER | But you can help me with the salad if you have time. |
| LENNY | Sure. Now? |
| MOTHER | Why not? (*exits*) |
| JACE | I'd be happy if my dad just remembered something. |

FATHER *enters, hands behind back.*

| | |
|---|---|
| FATHER | Okay, so guess which hand. |
| JACE | That one. |
| FATHER | Nope. Nothing here. Guess that's it then. |
| JACE | Oh, come on. |
| FATHER | All right, one more try. Guess again. |

JACE That one.

FATHER There you go.

*He reveals the car keys, jangling them.* JACE *grabs the keys.*

JACE Thanks, Dad.

FATHER (*tough*) You just keep one thing straight, kid.

JACE (*scared*) What?

FATHER Cars need gas. Be sure to put a couple bucks in.

JACE Sure thing.

FATHER And you think you could check the oil?

JACE No problem.

FATHER Thanks. I think it might be down a quart. Here's ten bucks.

JACE That's okay, I can cover it.

FATHER You take care of Lenny, I'll take care of the gas. It's your first date with her, show the girl a good time.

JACE All right.

FATHER Have a nice night.

JACE You too, Dad. (*starts to go*)

FATHER (*sternly*) Wait a minute.

| | |
|---|---|
| JACE | (*freezes*) What? |
| FATHER | I found my screwdriver. It was in the toolbox the whole time. (*winks at* JACE) See ya. (*exits*) |
| LENNY | That's what real life is like, isn't it? I mean, normal families live like that, don't they? |
| JACE | What's normal? Listen to the news. It's just like our parents—fighting, lying, covering up. How can anybody be normal when the whole world's a stupid mess? I stopped believing in normal when I stopped believing in Santa Claus. |
| LENNY | ...don't remind me of Christmas. |
| JACE | Your Christmases stink too, eh? |
| LENNY | I never know what to expect. |
| JACE | I do. Hell. |
| LENNY | Yeah, it's pretty bad. |
| JACE | How bad? |
| LENNY | Last year she passed out face down in the plum pudding. |
| JACE | My dad threw it at me. |
| LENNY | I bet he never knocked over the Christmas Tree. |
| JACE | No—but he puked on it. |
| LENNY | Really? |

JACE	Just before we opened the presents.

LENNY	Gross.

JACE	And then he wanted me to try on my new sweater.

LENNY	...I've never talked to anybody about this before. How come I can talk to you?

JACE	I don't know. I never talked to anybody about this stuff either.

LENNY	I feel kind of scared. Like I'm doing something wrong.

JACE	There's nothing wrong with talking.

LENNY	Unless you're in my house.

JACE	Same with mine.

LENNY	And at school, nobody talks.

JACE	Everybody talks—about nothing.

LENNY	You mean like boys and clothes and parties and school?

JACE	And cars and money and sex and drugs.

LENNY	I talk about that stuff, but that's not how I'm feeling inside. Inside I feel like I'm crazy.

JACE	Cause nobody talks about what's really going on.

LENNY — I'm always pretending everything's fine but I'm so scared. Sometimes I wonder why I'm alive. I feel completely useless.

JACE — There's nothing wrong with you. It's your parents who are useless. But I can see you. I can talk to you.

LENNY — ...I can talk to you too.

JACE — Yeah.

LENNY — Yeah.

*They kiss.*

I don't believe this.

JACE — What don't you believe?

LENNY — Everything. Meeting you. Being here. It seems too good to be true. Pinch me.

JACE — What?

LENNY — So I know it's real, it's not a dream.

JACE — You want me to pinch you? ...okay.

*He does.* LENNY *yells in pain.*

LENNY — Why'd you do it so hard!

JACE — Just following orders...so is this a dream or reality?

LENNY — I'm not sure. What do you think? (*pinches* JACE)

JACE — OWW! It's reality! Reality!

LENNY — ...so do you want to make a deal?

JACE — What kinda deal?

LENNY — If you have a problem, you can talk to me. And if I have one, I'll talk to you.

JACE — Not like our parents, eh?

LENNY — We'll really listen. We'll really talk.

JACE — You got it.

LENNY — Deal?

JACE — Deal.

*Pause. They start to kiss, but* LENNY *pulls away.*

LENNY — I better go now.

JACE — You can stay here if you want.

LENNY — I want to, but...

JACE — But what?

LENNY — I have to get home. I have to talk to them.

JACE — Why? Why go back there?

LENNY — I have to do something. Make them see.

JACE — It's a waste of time.

LENNY — I can help them change.

| | |
|---|---|
| JACE | Forget it. |
| LENNY | I can't, Jace. I have to try... Are you going to be all right here? |
| JACE | I'll manage. |
| LENNY | What do you mean, you'll manage? |
| JACE | I'll manage. |
| LENNY | You mean, if I go, you'll get high? |
| JACE | Maybe. |
| LENNY | Yes or no? |
| JACE | What do you think? |
| LENNY | Maybe I'd better not go. |
| JACE | That's no reason to stay. |
| LENNY | Why? I want to help you. |
| JACE | I don't need that kind of help. I'm not your mother. |
| LENNY | I know that. |
| JACE | If I get high it's my business. If you want to stay here to help yourself, fine. But don't think it's gonna change me somehow. You can't change me anymore than you can change your parents. Give it up. |
| LENNY | But I can't run away from it like you. And I won't stay high so I don't have to face it. |

JACE You just wanna be the perfect little daughter.

LENNY You're the perfect little son.

JACE What're you talking about?

LENNY You're a chip off the old block.

JACE No way! I'm not like him, I'll never be like him. Never.

LENNY But you are. You just use different drugs, that's all.

JACE I'm nothing like him. Nothing! You're the one who's gonna end up all teeth and furs and fancy clothes and drunk as a skunk in her five bedroom house. Not me. I'm never going back.

LENNY Jace, I have to go.

JACE Good. Go on. Go save 'em, Supergirl.

LENNY Goodnight.

JACE Watch out for the Kryptonite.

LENNY *exits.* JACE *reaches into his pack, pulls out a small bag.*

Up, up and away.

## Scene Ten

LENNY*'s home.*

| | |
|---|---|
| MOTHER | Hello, Darling, aren't you home early? |
| LENNY | I don't know, I don't think so. |
| MOTHER | It's only eleven o'clock. Weren't you having a good time? |
| LENNY | Yeah. |
| MOTHER | You can tell me. Didn't you like him? |
| LENNY | He's okay. Mom, I came home because I wanted to talk to you. |
| MOTHER | You know you can always talk to me, Darling. He upset you, didn't he? |
| LENNY | I don't want to talk about him, Mom, I want to talk about you. |
| MOTHER | You know you can tell me anything, honey. Did that boy do something to you? |
| LENNY | No. |
| MOTHER | But he upset you. |
| LENNY | He didn't do anything, Mom, it's you. |
| MOTHER | Me? |
| LENNY | Your drinking. |
| MOTHER | What drinking? |

LENNY — What drinking? You drink all the time, like before, tonight—when you were fighting with Dad you were drunk.

MOTHER — I was not drunk, I was upset.

LENNY — You were upset and you were drunk.

MOTHER — Leonore, tell me what you're going through. What's your problem?

LENNY — You, Mom, you. I'm worried sick about you. I keep thinking that I'm helping you but it never stops, you're just getting worse.

MOTHER — You are exaggerating. I don't have a problem. Most adults drink. It is a socially acceptable way to entertain, to relax.

LENNY — All the time?

MOTHER — In moderation.

LENNY — You don't drink in moderation, you're drunk all the time.

MOTHER — Am I drunk right now?

LENNY — Yes! No! All I know is it controls your life, it's killing you and I don't want you to die.

MOTHER — Leonore, don't worry, I'm not going to die. I know how much I drink. I regulate it. I am in complete control.

LENNY — Mom, that's just not true.

MOTHER — What is your problem, Leonore? Is it school?

LENNY Mom, you have every symptom of an alcoholic. You need help. We all need help.

MOTHER I think you might need some help, Leonore. I think you're being paranoid.

LENNY No, I'm not. I know what I live with. I know what's going on and it has to stop.

MOTHER What were you doing with that boy?

LENNY This has nothing to do with Jace.

MOTHER Let me see your eyes.

LENNY Why?

MOTHER Look at me! They're bloodshot. You've been doing drugs, haven't you? You've been smoking pot with that punk.

LENNY No I wasn't.

MOTHER Then why are your eyes like that? LSD?

LENNY Mom, we were just talking.

MOTHER You were just talking. About what? About me?

LENNY About a lot of things.

MOTHER Smoking dope and gossiping about your mother. What is happening to you?

LENNY It's not me, it's you!

DAD *enters.*

DAD What's all the commotion?

MOTHER We're having a little chat.

LENNY Dad, it's just gone too far. We've got to get some help. For Mom, for all of us.

DAD Help for what?

LENNY The drinking.

DAD Honey, it's late—

MOTHER Not too late to spread poison and lies. Not too late to come home high as a kite.

DAD You haven't been...?

LENNY No!

MOTHER She went out with that little drug addict and god only knows what they've been up to.

LENNY Dad, it's Mom's drinking, we've got to talk about Mom's drinking.

MOTHER She's never talked like this before. She must be on drugs.

DAD I don't know what's gotten into you, Leonore.

LENNY Nothing! This house! We've got to do something!

MOTHER I'll tell you what to do. You go sleep it off. Go to bed.

LENNY — I'm not going to bed till we do something about this.

MOTHER — Are you going to let her talk back to me?

DAD — Leonore, please.

LENNY — Dad.

DAD — And I was just starting to relax.

MOTHER — I don't want her seeing that little creep again. He's poison. If she even talks to that drug dealing snake she's grounded. For good.

LENNY — Why won't you listen to me?

DAD — Leonore, did you hear your mother?

LENNY — Did you hear me?

MOTHER — Go to bed.

LENNY — Mom. Dad.

DAD — Go to bed!

*Pause.*

LENNY *exits.*

## Scene Eleven

*The street.*

JACE *is panhandling.*

JACE

Spare change? Thank you very much. (*starts to limp*) Please sir, I can't afford the operation. Any amount will do. Thank you. (*still limping*) Ma'am, I swear it, a faith healer did this to me. He said "Be healed" and I've been lame ever since. ...same to you, turkeylips. (*sees another passerby*). Madam, invest in your child's future. For fifty cents I promise never to marry your daughter. Thank you. For another fifty cents I promise never to marry you. Thank you again.

LENNY *has entered and watches.* JACE *spots her, transforms into a hideous hunchback and hunches over to her.*

Foooood!

LENNY *is silent and uncomfortable.*

Feeeeeed meeeeee.

LENNY *reaches into her bag, pulls out a sandwich.* JACE *grabs it and wolfs it down. He finishes. He burps. Pause.*

Thanks.

*Pause.*

Long time no see. How ya doin?

LENNY So so...how come you haven't been in school?

JACE Been busy. Work.

LENNY Doing this?

JACE In the last two hours I made seventeen bucks. A boy's gotta eat. Minors can't get welfare, so here I am. Spare change?

LENNY You seem really hyper.

JACE I had a little pick-me-up.

LENNY Are you too stoned to talk to me?

JACE Of course not. I'm never too stoned.

LENNY I just...I'm sorry for the other night.

JACE Don't worry about it. Got another sandwich?

LENNY Sure. (*hands him another*)

JACE You make great sandwiches. This is umm delicious!

LENNY Jace, I really need to talk to you—

JACE What?

LENNY You were right about my parents.

JACE I was?

LENNY I can't help them, I have to help myself. I think we can both get help.

JACE Help for what?

LENNY I can't live this way anymore. I'd rather be dead.

JACE Maybe we already are.

LENNY No we're not, we have each other, we have...

JACE We have lots of things.

LENNY We can be there for each other.

JACE I'm here.

LENNY Come with me.

JACE Where?

LENNY To get help.

JACE Help for what? What's your problem?

LENNY Jace, please.

JACE Oh yeah, wait a minute—here comes a great riff!

JACE *turns the volume up on his walkman and now we hear it too.* JACE *starts playing air guitar along with Jimi Hendrix.* LENNY *watches for a bit, then grows impatient.*

LENNY Jace...Jace!

JACE *is lost in the music, totally shutting her out.*

Jace, I'm scared. I don't know what's going to happen. I thought we were friends, that we could help each other. But if I have to do it alone I will. The deal's still on, Jace. When you're ready.

*Pause.* JACE *continues with the music.* LENNY *starts to go.* JACE *turns and watches her go, wanting to stop her, but he can't.*

LENNY *exits.*

JACE *turns up the volume very loud, losing himself in the music. He turns his back to the audience, his head lowered. The music builds in volume.*

*The End.*